Extinct Monsters

Terror Bird

by Carol K. Lindeen

Reading Consultant:
Barbara J. Fox
Reading Specialist
North Carolina State University

Content Consultant:
Professor Timothy H. Heaton
Chair of Earth Science/Physics
University of South Dakota, Vermillion

Capstone
press®

Mankato, Minnesota

Blazers is published by Capstone Press,
151 Good Counsel Drive, P.O. Box 669, Mankato, Minnesota 56002.
www.capstonepress.com

Library of Congress Cataloging-in-Publication Data
Lindeen, Carol, 1976–
    Terror bird / by Carol K. Lindeen.
    p. cm.—(Blazers. Extinct monsters)
    Summary: "Simple text and illustrations describe phorusrhacos, how they
lived, and how they became extinct"—Provided by publisher.
    Includes bibliographical references and index.
    ISBN-13: 978-1-4296-0116-0 (hardcover)
    ISBN-10: 1-4296-0116-7 (hardcover)
    1. Phorusrhacos longissimus—South America—Juvenile literature.
2. Birds, Fossil—South America—Juvenile literature. 3. Paleontology—
Miocene—Juvenile literature. 4. Paleontology—South America—Juvenile
literature. I. Title. II. Series.
QE872.G8L56 2008
568'.3—dc22   2006038525

Editorial Credits
Jenny Marks, editor; Ted Williams, designer; Jon Hughes and Russell
    Gooday/www.pixelshack.com, illustrators; Wanda Winch, photo researcher

Photo Credits
Shutterstock/Galyna Andrushko, cover (background)
Valley Anatomical Preparations, Inc., 29 (skull)

1 2 3 4 5 6 12 11 10 09 08 07

Table of Contents

Chapter 1
The Ancient World................. 4

Chapter 2
A True Terror.......................... 8

Chapter 3
Fast and Fierce 16

Chapter 4
A Monster Disappears 22

Glossary 30
Read More................................. 31
Internet Sites............................. 31
Index 32

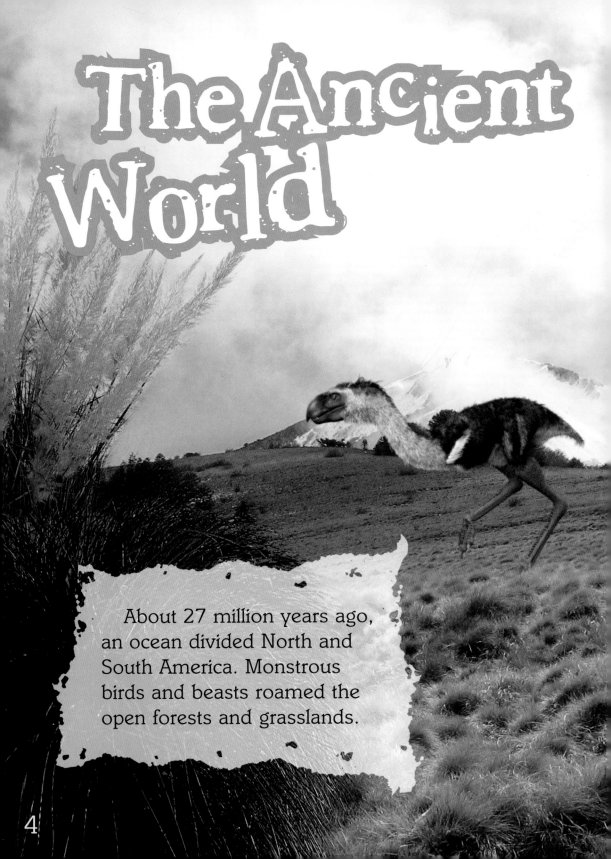

The Ancient World

About 27 million years ago, an ocean divided North and South America. Monstrous birds and beasts roamed the open forests and grasslands.

A bird called phorusrhacos (for-uhs-RAH-kuhs) ruled South America. No creature stood a chance against this meat-eater.

Monster Fact

The Phorusrhacos longissimus was one of many large, meat-eating terror birds.

A True Terror

The phorusrhacos was a powerful runner and a deadly hunter. This 8-foot (2.4-meter) monster weighed around 350 pounds (158 kilograms).

The phorusrhacos had a crushing jaw and an enormous beak. The bird stretched its long, strong neck to sink its beak into helpless prey.

Monster Fact

The phorusrhacos' beak looked much like an eagle's beak. The hooked tip was perfect for ripping meat.

Terror birds had light, hollow bones and long, muscled legs. Their top speed was a blazing 50 miles (80 kilometers) per hour.

The phorusrhacos had small wings but couldn't fly. Its wings were topped with a frightening claw. Terror birds may have used their claws to hunt or fight.

Fast and Fierce

A hunting terror bird chased its prey on foot. Phorusrhacos slammed its big beak into the prey to knock it to the ground.

Terror birds used their sharp beaks and pointed claws to rip food. They gulped down small animals whole.

Monster Fact

Scientists think terror birds
pounded small prey against
the ground to kill it.

The terror bird searched the grasslands for dead animals to eat. Sharp eyesight made it easy to spot a meal, dead or alive.

A Monster Disappears

About 2.5 million years ago, land formed between North and South America. Deadly beasts like the sabertooth cat traveled south.

Sabertooth cats soon
prowled the grasslands.
For the first time, the terror
birds had to fight for food.

With less and less food, the phorusrhacos began to disappear. Around 15,000 years ago, the giant terror bird became extinct.

Terror bird fossils are found in North and South America. You can see the fossils of these dangerous birds in museums.

Monster Fact

North American terror birds were called Titanis walleri.

terror bird skull

Glossary

extinct (ek-STINGKT)—no longer living; an extinct animal is one that has died out, with no more of its kind.

fossil (FOSS-uhl)—the remains or a trace of an animal or plant that is preserved in rock or in the earth

monstrous (MON-struss)—large and frightening

powerful (POW-uhr-full)—very strong

prey (PRAY)—an animal that is hunted by another animal for food

prowl (PROUL)—to move around quietly and secretly

Read More

Gunzi, Christiane. *The Best Book of Endangered and Extinct Animals*. Boston: Kingfisher, 2004.

Haines, Tim. *The Complete Guide to Prehistoric Life*. Buffalo, N.Y.: Firefly Books, 2006.

Zimmerman, Howard. *Beyond the Dinosaurs!: Sky Dragons, Sea Monsters, Mega-Mammals, and Other Prehistoric Beasts*. New York: Atheneum, 2001.

Internet Sites

FactHound offers a safe, fun way to find Internet sites related to this book. All of the sites on FactHound have been researched by our staff.

Here's how:
1. Visit *www.facthound.com*
2. Choose your grade level.
3. Type in this book ID **1429601167** for age-appropriate sites. You may also browse subjects by clicking on letters, or by clicking on pictures and words.
4. Click on the **Fetch It** button.

FactHound will fetch the best sites for you!

Index

beaks, 10, 16, 18
bones, 13

claws, 15, 18

extinction, 27, 28

fighting, 15
food, 18, 21, 24, 27
fossils, 28

habitats, 4
hunting, 8, 15, 16, 19

jaws, 10

legs, 13

necks, 10
North America, 4,
    23, 28

*Phorusrhacos
    longissimus*, 7

running, 8, 16

sabertooth cats, 23, 24
sight, 21
size, 8
South America, 4, 6, 23

Titanis walleri, 29
top speed, 13

wings, 15